Five Merseyside Moggies

by

R.M. Lewis

ALL AUTHOR'S PROCEEDS FROM THE SALE OF THIS BOOK GO TO HELP ILL-TREATED CATS.

Cat Illustrations by Lynzy West

First published 1988 by Countyvise Limited,
1 & 3 Grove Road, Rock Ferry, Birkenhead, Wirral, Merseyside L42 3XS.

Copyright   R.M. Lewis.
Photoset and printed by Birkenhead Press Limited,
1 & 3 Grove Road, Rock Ferry, Birkenhead, Merseyside L42 3XS.

ISBN 0 907768 22 9

All rights reserved. No part of this publication may be reproduced, stored in a retrieval system, or transmitted, in any form, or by any means, electronic, chemical, mechanical, photocopying, recording or otherwise, without the prior permission of the publisher.

Contents

Page

Introduction 4

Preface 5

1. Noddy of Birkenhead North 6

2. Guardian of the Ferry 8

3. The Bookworm 10

4. A Lover of Blooms 12

5. Mitzi of 'The Augustus John' 14

Postscript and Acknowledgements 16

Introduction

I can't remember when 'Nellie' first appeared. 'That cat' would sit, from time to time, on the garden wall, or miaow outside the window of whichever room had a light on. It was as persistent as a Double Glazing Salesman, and sent in regular orders for food and drink. On the arrival of a new puppy, she was taken to the vet's for a routine check-up and returned with unexpected information on her file. 'Herbert-Nellie', as he is now called, is very affectionate and appears at the side of the car seconds after arriving home however long or short the absence was. It is very tattyphilarious to find a cat has chosen to live with you and 'H.N.' is now a regular member of the team at Knotty Ash.

I hope you will enjoy reading about the adventures of five more Merseyside moggies, delightfully chronicled by R.M. Lewis.

Ken Dodd

Preface

While travelling regularly at all seasons, between Wirral and Liverpool, the writer passes the 'homes' of five friendly and interesting cats. The 'homes' of these animals are not the usual houses with the domestic comforts enjoyed by most pets, though sadly, not by all. These five cats live in public places though three have access to family quarters, but all have succeeded in influencing and training their guardians in providing them with food and shelter. The writer cannot honestly report that all the moggies repay this kind treatment by catching mice or rats, though one does — all are too fond of comfortable relaxation. However, the bond of affection between protector and protected is heartwarming to see, and winning a cat's affection is surely the best of repayment.

Observant readers will notice that the word 'owner' has not been used in this Preface. This is because, in some cases, there is a group ownership or shared ownership. It is to be hoped that the true stories of these five Merseyside moggies will give as much interest and pleasure to cat lovers (and perhaps stimulate cat-dislikers into appreciating the adaptability of felines) as the daily witnessing of one or other of these enchanting animals has given delight to the writer.

1. Noddy of Birkenhead North

To the surprise of the writer, Noddy is a lady. This is not her original name but was given her by courtesy of British Rail. Noddy's story begins when she became the pet of a family living in a street close to Birkenhead North Station. For five years Noddy lived in the same house, but her young life was plagued by unwelcome attacks from two local alsatians. The only place of safety for the frightened cat was a nearby wall. With the shrewdness and good sense common to cats, Noddy moved her quarters to the railway substation where the electrician kindly kept a watchful and affectionate eye on her for six years. He had little alternative because Noddy had adopted him and was certainly not returning to the misery of the wall and the watchful alsatians. From this time on, the light brown and white cat was known as Noddy.

At the end of the six years, Noddy, of her own will, moved the short distance to Birkenhead North Station where she shared the life and station routine of all the staff. The electrician continued to look after her, and for a further six years Noddy patrolled the station and, during bad weather, would share the mess-room with members of the staff. Sometimes she would sit with the electrician when it was his turn to be in the ticket-box, because railway personnel have to undertake all the work of running a station. Not only did Noddy supervise the selling of tickets but she kept a watchful eye on the arrival of trains from Liverpool. Many Merseysiders have been surprised to see this large, rather shaggy, gentle cat lying stretched out within inches of the coaches. She had become used to the noise of the trains, and true to cat nature, she made the alighting passengers walk round her. Sometimes, Noddy would crouch on the seat near the station entrance and observe the throng of people, or else she would gently doze yet be alert to any danger, particularly that of a passing dog.

The retirement of the electrician meant a change of guardian for Noddy. Very concerned that she be well looked after, he asked the present booking-office clerk if he would keep an eye on her. This, he willingly agreed to do being an animal lover, but neither he nor Noddy anticipated the publicity which was to come to both of them.

Being a self-contained cat, though friendly, Noddy would go upstairs in the mess-room for peace and quiet. Other railwaymen besides the staff of Birkenhead North, use the mess-room. One day, a telephone call from the manager of train crews reported that complaints had been made of an offensive smell in the mess-room where the men eat and hang their clothes, and Noddy was blamed. An ultimatum was issued that unless an alternative home was found for Noddy by the end of seven days then she must be destroyed.

There was consternation amongst the station staff, and Noddy's guardian, the present booking-office clerk, prepared for battle in defence of Noddy. First, he suggested that the unpleasant smell was probably from dead rats in the cellars of the mess-room. He then 'phoned the manager of train crews and said that an old cat if given another home, would not stay, but would return to the railway station. However, the manager was adamant, but he had not reckoned with the general public, for Noddy's protector had made sure that news of the ultimatum was published. Noddy's story appeared in the Echo, photographs of the animal, of her original and present guardians were published, and letters of anger and concern reached the office of the Daily Post and Echo from a roused public. Letters came from as far afield as Chester and North Wales. Radio Merseyside also helped in trying to obtain a reprieve for Noddy, and the determined booking-office clerk organised a petition in favour of reprieve. To his surprise, the interest of members of the public in Noddy was such that he obtained 530 signatures. All the publicity led to victory and Noddy was reprieved.

Recently, Noddy must have scratched her ear which became septic. A member of the public reported this fact to the R.S.P.C.A. and Noddy was taken to a vet in Seacombe. Her guardian gladly paid for Noddy's operation though this resulted in her losing part of the ear.

At the age of seventeen, Noddy is enjoying retirement in her old haunts of the railway station and mess-room. Her many friends send her tins of sardines in tomato sauce, or chicken, or beef. One lady from Wallasey regularly hands in a tin of cat food to the guard's van then at Birkenhead North the tin is delivered. There is truth in the statement of a young railway man to the writer that "Noddy is one of the best-fed cats on Merseyside." Single-eared but undefeated, Noddy still lies or sits on the platform awaiting the Liverpool trains.

2. Guardian of the Ferry

The Guardian of the Ferry is a cat of character. Named simply Cat or Kitty, her exact date of birth is unknown. She made her way at the age of seven or eight weeks to the Woodside Ferry, Birkenhead, and was accompanied by a large tortoiseshell lady friend who was definitely not her mother. It is probable that both animals had come from the yards of nearby Western Ship Repairers or from the Lairage, the home of many strays. Both animals would eat together but Kitty would butt her friend away from the dish so that she could have more for herself. The tortoiseshell lady had lost her miaow but she gave a good hiss. Such treatment from an impudent kitten was unbearable so the tortoiseshell lady departed for more comfortable facilities leaving Kitty the undisputed Guardian of the Ferry.

There has always been a cat at Woodside but none has made such an impact on the staff or the public as Kitty. Not only is she noticed by passengers sailing across the Mersey to Liverpool, but several stop to take her photograph. Some years ago, an old lady brought thirty pence a week for Kitty's food, and tins of cat food are often handed in by kindly passengers. When the staff decided to have Kitty doctored, another old lady brought a basket, rather like that used for pigeons, so that Kitty could have easy transport. Previous to her visit to the vet, Kitty had produced four litters of kittens. Fortunately, homes were found for all the offspring except one. This poor little creature was attacked by a rat.

Kitty is not a good 'ratter' as one might expect, nor is she too expert in catching mice unless she really needs to do so. However, there was one amusing occasion when the collector-inspector was standing near the mess-room with Kitty at his side. To his amazement, a mouse appeared and sat washing its whiskers at Kitty's side. He turned to the cat and said, "There's a mouse!" and Kitty, seeing it for the first time, grabbed it.

Four years ago Kitty was lost. The ferry is constantly manned except at night and during the Christmas bank holidays. Returning after the Christmas break the members of the staff were upset at not finding any sign of Kitty. She was lost for ten days, and it seems likely that she was accidentally locked in the nearby Lairage where she would live on mice and birds. Occasionally, birds fly into the ferry buildings and Kitty sits watching them and moving her lips in hopeful anticipation.

Kitty has her mad moments and is particularly agile. She has made the ferry her home for about seven and a half years so she is in the prime of life. The only upset to her happy and contented existence has been the building of the new terminal. She has lost some of her old resting places and several of her climbing sprees have necessarily ended. However, she has benefited by now having splendid new living conditions. The two lady members of the ferry staff have brought her a new feeding bowl, and Kitty is far less dusty than she was in the old building. She loves to sit on paper, particularly crisp packets, and when the builders left cement with a board on top, Kitty found this an excellent resting place. Throughout months of disturbance owing to the alterations, Kitty never strayed, but kept loyal to her good-hearted guardians, and she was present at the opening ceremony of the new ferry terminal.

This cat of character is certainly game. Only recently she stalked a fox which visited the ferry, and she holds her ground in the faces of the variety of dogs travelling across the river. A regular dog passenger, an alsatian called Prince, has had his nose slapped for some misdemeanour. Now he walks very circumspectly past Kitty.

Though the ferry is closed at night, Kitty finds ways of getting outside unless she wishes to sleep in her warm cardboard box. She is not inclined to walk down to the river though once, during the alterations, she had to be down there. Sitting watching the water, she dozed and nearly fell in. This well-fed cat with her dislike of fish and chicken and her passion for liver, is devoted to the staff who have befriended her. She will often follow the ladies into the nearby car park, or follow the collector-inspector to the Woodside Hotel so that he has to chase her home. Her welcome of the staff at six in the morning shows her affection for them, though admittedly, there are days when she chooses to stay in bed. As Guardian of the Ferry, Kitty is free to choose what she does, whether to sleep or prowl, and certainly the devoted staff are completely under her paw.

3. The Bookworm

Sam is not a Scouser. In fact, he was born a Southerner but belongs to Liverpool by adoption. Nothing is known of his original home because he is a stray, but despite hardships in his kittenhood, Sam has fallen on his paws by choosing a fine home.

Sam's story begins in Swindon where his present owner lived, and being an animal lover, he was concerned to hear about a stray ginger kitten crossing dangerous roads. A severe Winter set in with heavy snow and anxiety for the stray increased. Eventually, as his owner says, "He found us, and we found him." Advertisements were put in the local paper, the police were told, but nobody claimed the ginger tom. This was strange because the animal was house-trained. So he was adopted and given the name of Sam. Unfortunately, Sam was run over while living in Swindon and ever since has had a fear of cars which, for him now in a busy city, is a good thing. He has certainly lost two or three of his nine lives with the experiences of his youth.

Sam's owner came to Liverpool, and the cat was transported by car. He was happy in the car, though not outside it because of his understandable fear. Wrapped up in blankets inside the cat-basket he found the journey no problem at all. Sam quickly settled in Liverpool though he missed the garden in Swindon where he could roam freely. At first, he lived near the Anglican Cathedral and would be put on a lead and taken for walks in the Cathedral precinct, but later his owner opened a bookshop near the city centre.

Sam's new home became the bookshop because the family lives there. At the age of eight, Sam is young and agile enough to thoroughly enjoy roaming over the house and in the shop. He never ventures out of the shop door because it opens onto the main road, but he is able to take his exercise at the back. Three years ago, a she-cat named Ruby came to share Sam's home. At first, he was annoyed, but now he puts up with her and the two enjoy each other's company. Ruby was nearly lost on one occasion when the D.H.S.S. left a nearby building which is a large, rambling hall. It was a job to find her, but the little cat had the good sense to knock from the inside of the window and so was rescued. Sam was glad to be reunited with his friend.

Both cats are fed together but neither likes fish — in fact, Sam is sick if he is offered fish. He loves chicken or beef, and wisely has his milk with water.

Sam is a sensible cat and appreciates the goodness of his owners. Life for him is delightful, especially when he can be among the books, but there is one important rule which he knows he must keep — on no account must he sit or lie on a book. Paw marks on books are not appreciated by customers. Otherwise, the bookworm is free to roam, laze or sleep amongst the books as he pleases.

4. A Lover of Blooms

Thomas Catt shares his life with two alsatians and another cat, and most of his time he is surrounded by flowers. In case the reader detects a spelling error, let him understand that 'Thomas Catt' is inscribed on the disc attached to Thomas's collar, and so is the name of the florist to whom he belongs. There is a shared ownership of Thomas as his story will reveal.

The origin of Thomas is unknown but he had been injured before he found his way, as a small kitten, to the florist's shop. He is perfectly fit now and remarkably spry for his fifteen years. The present owners of the shop who inherited Thomas eight years ago find that the sound of a banging drum frightens him and he runs and hides. Perhaps his injury occurred during a march in the city when he was a kitten.

When the original owner of the florist's shop adopted the semi-Persian black and white kitten she named him Thomas Catt. She already had a cat named Tiger and surprisingly, the two animals settled amicably except that Tiger, beautifully striped but lazy, would not allow Thomas upstairs. When the original owner retired eight years ago she took Tiger with her and left Thomas with the new owners. However, Thomas had to share his floral home with two alsatians and another cat named Gene. All the animals get on well together in the shop, but the dogs will not put up with the cats at home, so Thomas sleeps during the week upstairs where he can now go, and where he is warm. He sees little of Gene because a cat is required at another branch of the florist's in one of the suburbs.

A lady in a nearby street who loves animals takes Thomas for the weekends or during holiday periods. She spoils and indulges him and Thomas realises that he can wind her round his paw. Transport to and from his second home can be by van, or by being carried in a shopping basket with just his head peeping out. Sometimes he is carried bodily and upon returning, once safely over the busy main road, he is given his freedom. He knows the shop and runs eagerly towards it. Now that the lady has retired, Thomas sometimes stays longer than a weekend.

When it is feeding time all the animals play by the rules. They queue up, are fed individually but at the same time. Then they agree to differ and each goes to his or her own corner. Any of Thomas's food remaining is quickly eaten by the two alsatians. Thomas enjoys gourmet food at the weekends but has to be content with fewer luxuries in the shop where there are other animals to feed.

In the Summer the shop is often open and Thomas will wander out, but he does not go far. The problem is that, like most cats, he enjoys sitting under parked cars and there are many by the shop. He is an independent cat yet he enjoys company. When he lived with Tiger he could be bad-tempered and use his claws, but he has mellowed over the years and is friendly. Like all cats, Thomas enjoys warmth, so his favourite spot is to lie in the window amongst the blooms. He will lie for hours stretched out, and some passers-by have thought he was a woolly toy! Thomas is certainly attractive as he sprawls in the window. He does not damage the plants for he is graceful, but he occasionally nibbles the spider-plants and leaves his long hairs in the window.

Thomas is one of the fortunate cats and leads a life of leisure. He is popular with customers and children. Incredible though it seems, his present owner was offered £400 for Thomas. "It's more than my life's worth to take £4,000!" was the reply. Not many cats receive an offer like that.

5. Mitzi of the 'Augustus John'

Few cats can boast of having been born in one of Liverpool's oldest pubs — The Crown, Lime Street, or perhaps it would be more accurate to say 'on the roof of The Crown' for that is what happened. A mother cat gave birth to her kittens on the roof of The Crown Public House and Mitzi was the last of the litter.

The licencee of the nearby American Bar, also in Lime Street, had just lost his pet cat so the newly-born kitten was offered as a replacement and was described as being a she-cat. Consequently, she was named Mitzi. Her appearance has been described as 'wet, and just like a bag of chicken bones.' Three months later, Mitzi had an appointment with the vet. "Why have you brought this cat to me?" he asked. "There won't be any kittens because Mitzi is a tom!" It was too late to change the name for the animal answered to Mitzi.

Mitzi has moved around and experienced life in four city public houses, and this semi-Persian white cat with a ginger saddle has become very well-known and popular. Patrons of the American Bar are cosmopolitan and seamen from all over the world have admired Mitzi and taken photographs of him. Leo from the Philippines took several photos some of which he took home with him. There are photos of Mitzi in many other parts of the world besides the Philippines.

One patron was a Canadian set designer at a city theatre. He noticed Mitzi's habit of lying on a canopy behind the bar. As the cat slept he would stretch one paw out. Each night, the Canadian would hang his hat on the extended paw! A skylight was above the bar and Mitzi liked, occasionally, to climb through this when it was open. Nearby, in those days, were some Chinese restaurants. Mitzi would make for the backyards, catch a rat, then climb back through the skylight. One can imagine the feelings of patrons, especially the girls, when they saw Mitzi descending with a live rat in his jaws.

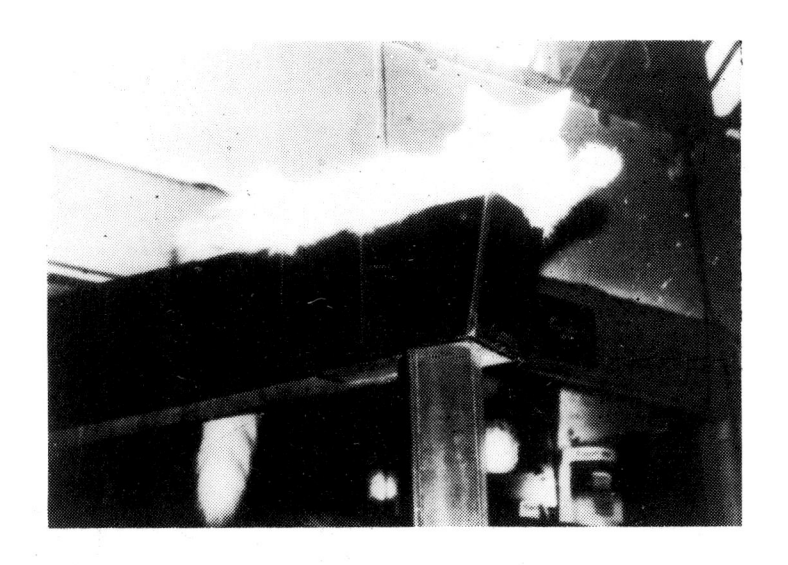

Mitzi is a most entertaining cat and since his owners moved to The Augustus John, in the heart of the University complex, his admirers have become more numerous. Old customers from the American Bar come up to The Augustus John 'just to see Ginger' as they fondly call him. The students who patronise the well known public house all love Mitzi and call him 'Garfield' after a character in The Echo. The veterinary students are particularly interested. Everybody makes a fuss of this beautiful cat especially when he sits on top of the bar in order to receive acclaim and admiration.

Well-fed with his daily food and numerous tit-bits, Mitzi enjoys a wide variety of offerings but is particularly partial to cheese, yoghourt, crabmeat and prawns. He likes Dairylee triangles of cheese provided one holds the piece for him — not otherwise. He also prefers water to milk and has his own pint pot. It is essential that the water contains ice-cubes. He will not drink it without. He even pushes the top off the bucket containing ice-cubes, so eager is he for them. Oddly, Mitzi prefers the water in which fish is boiled rather than the fish, and he'll leave sardines but thoroughly enjoys the oil.

Like his fellow-tom at the florist's, Mitzi enjoys sitting or lying on the window-sill of the bar parlour. He loves the warmth of the sun and to nibble the juiciest parts of the ornamental plants. At eleven years of age, Mitzi is in the prime of life and is likely to give pleasure to many more people. He is a real 'pub character'.

Mitzi of 'The Augustus John'

Postscript

The true life stories of these five Merseyside moggies warms the hearts of cat lovers, for this is how all cats should be treated. There is a thread running throughout the five stories — that of concern, care and affection for the animals on the part of the guardians or owners. These simple stories reflect the true nature of the people of Merseyside — warm and friendly. Men and women who are prepared to put themselves out to adopt a 'stray', not a selected or chosen animal, are people of integrity and humanity.

Acknowledgements

The writer wishes to thank all those who generously gave of their time in supplying information about their animals.

Thanks are due to the cats, too, for the enjoyment of their company during the interviews, and for the pleasure given to the writer through unexpected glimpses of them over the years.

This booklet is dedicated to Noddy who died a few days after completion of her life-story.